Carolyn's Lit. Guide

Adventures

5 - 6 Grade

By Carolyn Oravitz

Fun, Fantastic, Fantabulous Books to Read and Enjoy!

LITERATURE GUIDES

With Chapter Questions and End of the Book

ISBN: 0997197235
ISBN-13: 978-0-9971972-3-5

ACKNOWLEDGEMENTS

Robinson Crusoe by Daniel Defoe, Classic Starts (retold from the original), Sterling Publishing

Oliver Twist by Charles Dickens, Great Illustrated Classics, Baronet Books

The Lion, the Witch and the Wardrobe by C. S. Lewis, Scholastic

A Christmas Carol by Charles Dickens, Great Illustrated Classic, Baronet Books

20,000 Leagues Under the Sea by Jules Verne, Great Illustrated Classics, Baronet Books

Dark Enough to See the Stars by Cindy Noonan, Helping Hands Press

Parent/Teacher Information

Carolyn's Lit. Guide Adventures

List of benefits:

These literature guides have been designed as supplemental materials to aid the student in building reading skills.

The grade level books have been carefully selected and have been proven to be of great interest to students, helping motivate the most reluctant reader as well as those children who enjoy and excel at reading. Some of these books are abridged or adapted versions of classics that introduce students to timeless themes, plots, and characters. These versions help the child develop a love for reading while improving his or her reading skills. Children may choose to read the unabridged version of the same book after reading the abridged one.

Each fun, yet educational, set of books contain multiple-choice chapter questions to work on while reading. Each set also has an and end of the book open-book test with 25 multiple-choice questions to take after the book has been carefully read and the chapter questions have been checked, corrected, and studied.

Easy to follow independent work and students will only need assistance when the questions and tests have been completed. Parent/teacher answers are provided with chapter numbers to follow up.

Book sets come in Grades 3 and 4, Grades 5 and 6, and Grades 7 and 8.

Books can be found on Amazon and other websites where books are sold.

Student Instructions: Read these fun, fantastic, fantabulous books from the list above and then answer the chapter questions. After you have carefully read each book and have had your chapter question answers checked, take the end of the book test. Then have your teacher or parent check your answers.

Contents

LITERATURE GUIDE ONE

Robinson Crusoe

by Daniel Defoe

Chapter Questions

Student Instructions: Read the book and answer the questions as you finish each chapter. If you need help, you may look in the book for help.

1. Robinson's parents didn't want him to become a sailor, but he felt it was his destiny. What did he mean by his destiny? _____ (Chapter 1)

   A. something that had to happen

   B. his punishment

   C. his reward

2. What happened to Robinson during his first voyage? _____ (Chapter 2)

   A. He caught salmon and bass.

   B. He became seasick.

   C. He found his missing brother.

3. The captain of the ship, John's father, suggested this was the cause of their shipwreck._____ (Chapter 3)

   A. Their ship wrecked because Robinson ignored his father's wishes.

   B. Their ship wrecked because a killer whale was lurking below the ship.

   C. Their ship wrecked because there was too much weight on the ship.

4. On Robinson's second voyage to Africa, pirates entered their ship and did this. _____ (Chapter 5)

   A. They shared their adventure stories and became Robinson's friends.

   B. They took Robinson as a slave.

   C. They freed the prisoners who were aboard.

5. What two things happened that caused Robinson to think about escaping? _____ (Chapter 6)

   A. His master had a sturdy boat and planned a fun evening on the boat for some friends.

   B. His master had a strong horse and let Robinson ride on it.

   C. His master went on a long trip and let Robinson have two weeks off from work.

6. Who rescued Robinson and Xury? _____ (Chapter 8)

    A. a ship sailing to Brazil

    B. a ship sailing to Australia

    C. a ship sailing to Mexico

7. Robinson became a plantation owner. What is a plantation? _____ (Chapter 9)

    A. a ship factory

    B. a large sailing ship

    C. a large farm

8. How many survived when Robinson's shipwrecked? _____ (Chapter 12)

    A. four including Robinson

    B. one, only Robinson

    C. about a dozen

9. Robinson was able to get some of these supplies from the ruined ship. _____ (Chapter 12)

    A. biscuits, rope, clothes, and a dog

    B. wheat, a pillow, a cat, and a dog

    C. a clock, a radio, and a dog

10. After realizing he and a dog were alone on the island, Robinson decided he needed to do this. _____ (Chapter 14)

    A. He needed to build a more permanent shelter.

    B. He needed to spend most of his time in high trees, looking for passing ships.

    C. He needed to send a note in a bottle into the ocean water.

11. Robinson wanted to keep track of time, so he started a calendar on this. _____ (Chapter 14)

    A. a carved board he salvaged from the wrecked ship

    B. the wall of the cave

    C. a big tree by the beach

12. Some of these activities kept Robinson busy on the island. _____
(Chapter 15)

    A. hunting animals for sport and using a coconut to play games with the dog

    B. making a chair and a table and hunting animals for food

    C. writing fictional stories, hoping to sell them after he was rescued

13. Robinson discovered some of these on the island. _____ (Chapter 16)

    A. pumpkins and corn

    B. grapes, melons, and oranges

    C. more dogs and baboons

14. Robinson discovered there were only two seasons on the island. They were _____ (Chapter 17)

    A. fall and summer

    B. snowy and sunny

    C. rainy and dry

15. Robinson got a new pet. It was _____ (Chapter 17)

    A. a parrot

    B. a pony

    C. a pig

16. After Robinson planted crops, he did this. _____ (Chapter 18)

    A. He had his watchdog protect them.

    B. He built a fence around them.

    C. He shared them with nearby animals.

17. Robinson spent four months working on his boat— his canoe—but there was a problem. What was the problem? _____ (Chapter 19)

    A. It was too heavy to move.

    B. Termites ate a hole in it.

    C. He had no cloth to make sails.

18. Robinson was now on the island ten years. How had he changed? _____ (Chapter 21)

   A. He lost 50 pounds.

   B. He gained weight from eating chocolate from the cocoa trees.

   C. He had long hair, a long beard, and sunburned skin.

19. Robinson found a big footprint in the sand. How did he react? _____ (Chapter 22)

   A. He searched everywhere and was so glad someone was there with him.

   B. He was afraid natives would come and destroy his camp and kill him.

   C. He thought the footprint belonged to a gorilla because it was so large.

20. After Robinson was on the island for over twenty years, another ship wrecked near his island. What did he find on the ship? _____ (Chapter 24)

   A. another dog

   B. some frightened children

   C. three surviving sailors

21. Robinson met another person, and they became friends. His name was Friday because of this. _____ (Chapter 25)

   A. Robinson found him on a Friday.

   B. Friday was the only English word the native could speak.

   C. He was born on a Friday.

22. Friday and Robinson became good friends, and they had this in common. _____ (Chapter 26)

   A. They both longed for a life of adventure and left home against their father's wishes.

   B. They both were orphaned at an early age.

   C. They both had a goal of going to Canada.

23. Robinson and Friday worked well together and decided to build this. _____ (Chapter 27)

    A. a sturdy fort

    B. a new boat

    C. a lookout tower to watch for rescuers

24. Robinson and Friday helped Captain Walsh overcome villains, so the captain offered to do this for them. _____ (Chapter 29)

    A. Captain Walsh offered to take them back to England.

    B. Captain Walsh offered to bring women to the island, so they could each have a wife.

    C. Captain Walsh offered to give them farm tools to help them grow more crops.

25. Robinson finally made it back home and found out this happened while he was gone. _____ (Chapter 30)

    A. His parents had another son, so he had a younger brother.

    B. His parents disowned him out of anger.

    C. His parents had died while he was gone.

Student, when you've checked and corrected all your answers in this literature guide, and you've read every page in the book, then take the End of the Book Test.

You can find the answers to these questions on page 96.

Robinson Crusoe

by Daniel Defoe

End of the Book Test

Student Instructions: Student, each question is worth 4 points. Let's see how well you've read this book. You may use this as an open book test and complete it within a 30-minute time limit. After you take the test, have your teacher/parent score the test for you. Then correct the wrong answers by reviewing the book for the correct answers.

1. Robinson Crusoe is written in what point of view? _____ (Chapter 1)

    A. first person - I, me, my

    B. second person - you, your

    C. third person - he/she, him/her

2. Robinson Crusoe is considered classic literature. Classic means ____ (Chapter 1)

    A. humorous

    B. nonfiction

    C. popular and timeless

3. Why didn't Robinson Crusoe's parents want him to go to sea? _____ (Chapter 1)

    A. His father was a doctor, and he wanted Robinson to be a doctor too.

    B. They previously lost two other sons.

    C. They wanted him to stay home and marry the mayor's daughter.

4. Robinson craved adventure. Craved means _____ (Chapter 1)

    A. had a strong desire for

    B. disliked intensely

    C. avoided

5. On a ship, the sailors slept in a hammock. A hammock is _____ (Chapter 2)

    A. a hanging canvas bed

    B. a bunk bed

    C. a bed large enough for three sailors

6. Robinson became seasick on his first voyage. What does seasick mean? _____ (Chapter 2)

    A. sick because the ship's cook made bad-tasting food

    B. sick and jealous because he couldn't catch any fish at sea

    C. sick because the waves tossed the ship up and down, over and over again

7. Robinson's ship was shipwrecked because of _____ (Chapter 11)

    A. hitting a sandbar

    B. hitting an iceberg

    C. hitting a large whale

8. Personification is giving human qualities to something that is not human. Which of the following is an example of personification in this story? _____ (Chapter 11)

    A. The waves grabbed me in their clutches.

    B. The waves were as high as palm trees.

    C. The waves were blue with white tips.

9. Robinson said, "For all my bad luck, it seems I had one very real talent …." What did he say his talent was? _____ (Chapter11)

    A. shipbuilding

    B. survival

    C. farming

10. Robinson screamed at the top of his lungs because of this. _____ (Chapter 12)

    A. He was stung by a scorpion.

    B. He hoped someone would hear him.

    C. He realized he was the only survivor of the shipwreck.

11. Robinson found thirty pounds worth of gold on the ruined ship and did this. _____ (Chapter 13)

    A. He left it there because there was no place for him to spend it.

    B. He took it with him even though there was no place to spend it on the island.

    C. He melted it and made it into pans for himself.

12. What did Robinson think was the most important part of his life now that he was abandoned on the island? _____ (Chapter14)

   A. to be safe from any wild animals or natives

   B. to try to find maps

   C. to search for more gold

13. While living on the island, Robinson learned he could make anything as long as he did this. _____ (Chapter 15)

   A. as long as he had the right materials

   B. as long as he had someone helping him

   C. as long as he set his mind to it

14. After being on the island for so long, Robinson's thinking changed, and he started thinking this way about it. _____ (Chapter 16)

   A. The island was his home and not a place where he was trapped.

   B. The island was probably a British territory and might have friendly inhabitants.

   C. The island was slowly sinking into the sea.

15. What did Robinson learn about planting seeds? _____ (Chapter 17)

   A. Plant seeds right after the rainy season ended.

   B. Plant them close to the ocean.

   C. Plant them in the rainy season.

16. How did Robinson solve the problem of birds and hares eating his crops? _____ (Chapter 18)

   A. He hung feathers all around and built a fence.

   B. He made poison for the animals.

   C. He shot them whenever they came near.

17. Robinson's most prized possession was this. _____ (Chapter 19)

    A. his rifle

    B. his chair

    C. his umbrella

18. Robinson heard a strange voice call him out of his sleep. The voice said, "Where were you? How did you get here?" It was the voice of _____ (Chapter 20)

    A. a native

    B. his parrot

    C. an angel calling him

19. A decade had passed, and Robinson was still on the island. A decade is _____ (Chapter 21)

    A. ten years

    B. twenty years

    C. a dozen years

20. Because he was so afraid of the footprint, in a fit of craziness Robinson decided to do this. _____ (Chapter 22)

    A. Rip up all his crops and set his goats free.

    B. Light a bonfire, hoping any passing ship would find him.

    C. Get in his small boat and flee the island.

21. Something scared Robinson to his "bare bones." It was _____ (Chapter 23)

    A. a bear and her cubs

    B. an alligator with sharp teeth

    C. a sick, old billy goat

22. After Robinson had been alone for over twenty years, he finally met someone who became his friend. Who was his friend? _____ (Chapter 25)

    A. a monkey, who seemed almost human

    B. a British sailor, who was also shipwrecked

    C. an escaped prisoner

23. Robinson and Friday spent their days in a routine. What was the first thing they did each day? _____ (Chapter 26)

    A. Robinson taught Friday how to speak English.

    B. They worked on the farm.

    C. They checked the island to make sure the natives did not return.

24. Robinson and Friday were finally able to return to England on a ship. What was the name of the captain? _____ (Chapter 29)

    A. Captain Walsh

    B. Captain Morgan

    C. Captain Pace

25. When Robinson finally returned home, he noticed these changes. _____ (Chapter 30)

    A. The town was smaller because many buildings had been torn down.

    B. The town was bigger and busier.

    C. The town had a welcome-home parade for him.

You can find the answers to these questions on page 97.

LITERATURE GUIDE TWO

Oliver Twist
by Charles Dickens

Chapter Questions

Student Instructions: Read the book and answer the questions as you finish each chapter. If you need help, you may look in the book for help.

1. Oliver Twist was an orphan because of this. _____ (Chapter 1)

   A. His mother died when he was born.

   B. His father abandoned him.

   C. Both parents died in a train wreck.

2. A simile compares two things with the words like or as. Oliver looked like a bag of bones is a simile, and it means this. _____ (Chapter 2)

   A. He was lumpy.

   B. He was very, very thin.

   C. He looked like he ate bones.

3. Fagin and his gang of boys taught Oliver this. _____ (Chapter 3)

   A. how to take things out of other people's pockets

   B. how to smoke clay pipes

   C. how to cook sausages

4. Oliver finally realized this about Fagin and his gang. _____ (Chapter4)

   A. They were great guys.

   B. They were thieves who stole from people's pockets.

   C. They were interested in playing chess.

5. Mr. Brownlow and his family took great care of Oliver, but trouble happened when _____ (Chapter 5)

   A. Oliver stole some books.

   B. Oliver wanted to go back to Fagin and his gang.

   C. Fagin had Nancy and Bill Sikes kidnap Oliver and bring him back to Mr. Brownlow.

6. Mr. Bumble brought what bad news about Oliver? _____ (Chapter 6)

   A. He said Oliver attacked a boy and ran away.

   B. He said Oliver had a deadly illness.

   C. He said Oliver's mother wanted him to come home.

7. Oliver is forced to help rob a house, and he does this. _____ (Chapter 7)

    A. He steals some toys for himself and his friends.

    B. He steals watches for Fagin and his gang.

    C. He does not want to steal and gets shot when he tries to warn the homeowners.

8. A dying, old lady said she stole something from Oliver's mother. What did she steal? _____ (Chapter 8)

    A. gold

    B. a fur coat

    C. a valuable painting

9. Monks had a purpose for Oliver. He wanted this to happen to Oliver. _____ (Chapter 9)

    A. Monks wanted Oliver to die from the gunshot wound.

    B. Monks wanted Oliver to be sent to prison for life.

    C. Monks wanted Oliver to be his junior partner.

10. Why did Mr. Bumble ask Mrs. Corney to marry him? _____ (Chapter 10)

    A. He thought she was pretty.

    B. He was lonely.

    C. He thought she had valuables and money.

11. Oliver survived his gunshot wound. Who took care of him until he was healthy again? _____ (Chapter 11)

    A. Mrs. Maylie and Rose Maylie

    B. Mrs. Corney and Mr. Bumble

    C. Fagin and the Dodger

12. Rose Maylie was a very kind person. Harry loved her and wanted to marry her, but she said he should not marry her because of this. _____ (Chapter 12)

    A. She did not have a good background.

    B. She was in love with someone else.

    C. She was too sick.

13. Monks wanted to get information about this. _____ (Chapter 13)

    A. Monks wanted to know about Oliver's gunshot wound.

    B. Monks wanted to see if Oliver was stealing.

    C. Monks wanted to know about the death of Oliver's mother.

14. Monks finally got what used to belong to Oliver's mother. It was a gold locket with this name on it. _____ (Chapter 14)

    A. Mrs. Corney

    B. Agnes

    C. Monks

15. Oliver had an older brother who tried to get him into prison. His brother was _____ (Chapter 15)

    A. Mr. Bumble

    B. Fagin

    C. Monks

16. Oliver found Mr. Brownlow and was able to do this. _____ (Chapter 16)

    A. Oliver explained he was not a thief.

    B. Oliver stole his wallet.

    C. Oliver gave him some gold.

17. Noah Claypole and Charlotte were thieves, and this person wanted them to steal for him. _____ (Chapter 17)

    A. Fagin

    B. Monks

    C. Oliver

18. This person was arrested for being a pickpocket. _____ (Chapter 18)

    A. Fagin

    B. Oliver

    C. the Dodger

19. Nancy wanted to go out at 11:00 at night to meet Rose Maylie. She couldn't because _____ (Chapter 19)

    A. she was too tired.

    B. Sikes wouldn't let her leave.

    C. she forgot.

20. How old was Oliver's older brother Monks? _____ (Chapter 20)

    A. 20

    B. 25

    C. 28

21. Nancy was murdered as a result of this. _____ (Chapter 21)

    A. Noah Claypole told Sikes Nancy didn't love him.

    B. Nancy betrayed him.

    C. Nancy told Mr. Brownlow and Rose about Monks.

22. In chapter twenty-two, we learn this about Monks. _____ (Chapter 22)

    A. Monks didn't want to share his inheritance with his brother Oliver.

    B. Monks was a murderer.

    C. Monks escaped back to Fagin.

23. Sikes tried to escape by doing this. _____ (Chapter 23)

    A. hiding in a closet

    B. climbing on the roof

    C. slipping out the back door

24. Oliver would only get his inheritance if he did this. _____ (Chapter 24)

    A. never married

    B. never had children

    C. never broke the law

25. Oliver Twist ends this way. _____ (Chapter 25)

    A. Oliver received half of his father's property, and Mr. Brownlow adopted him.

    B. Oliver Twist went back to live a life of crime.

    C. Oliver Twist saved Fagin and all his gang from prison.

Student, when you've checked and corrected all your answers in this literature guide and you've read every page in the book, then take the End of the Book Test.

You can find the answers to these questions on page 98.

Oliver Twist

by Charles Dickens

End of the Book Test

Student Instructions: Student, each question is worth 4 points. Let's see how well you've read this book. You may use this as an open book test and complete it within a 30-minute time limit. After you take the test, have your teacher/parent score the test for you. Then correct the wrong answers by reviewing the book for the correct answers.

1. The author's purpose is the reason for the written work of fiction or nonfiction. What was the author's purpose in Oliver Twist? _____

    A. to entertain

    B. to inform

    C. to persuade

2. "Fact" means true and unchanging. "Opinion" means how I feel about something. The sentence "Oliver Twist was the best book ever written about orphans" is _____

    A. a fact

    B. an opinion

3. Why was Oliver so poor? _____ (Chapter 1)

    A. His mother died when he was born.

    B. His parents gambled away their fortune.

    C. His parents spent all their money on useless items.

4. Why did Oliver hit Noah? _____ (Chapter 2)

    A. Noah hit him first.

    B. Noah stole his money.

    C. Noah insulted his mother.

5. Why did Oliver run away to London? _____ (Chapter 3)

    A. He liked big cities.

    B. He wanted to hide from Mr. Bumble and other mean people.

    C. He went looking for his family.

6. When Oliver realized Fagin and his gang were thieves, he did this. _____ (Chapter 4)

    A. He wanted to steal too.

    B. He was shocked and didn't want to steal.

    C. He grabbed a lady's purse and took the money.

7. What was Oliver's act of bravery? _____ (Chapter 7)

    A. He alerted the sleeping family even though he knew it could result in his death.

    B. He grabbed a gun and shot the bad guys.

    C. He ran away to a new city.

8. The dying old lady, Sally, regretted her actions for this reason. _____ (Chapter 8)

    A. She never got married.

    B. Oliver's mother trusted her, and she let her down.

    C. She wanted to adopt Oliver.

9. Why did Monks think the robbery was unsuccessful? _____ (Chapter 9)

    A. The robbery wasn't planned well.

    B. There weren't enough valuables in the house.

    C. The windows in the house were broken, and someone else already robbed it.

10. When Mr. Bumble said, "I'll do it," what did he mean? _____ (Chapter 10)

    A. He would join Fagin's gang.

    B. He would contact Oliver.

    C. He would ask Mrs. Corney to marry him.

11. After Oliver woke up from his gunshot wound, he went to this house for help. _____ (Chapter 11)

    A. Fagin's house

    B. the house they tried to rob

    C. a stranger's house

12. Harry Maylie loved Rose for this amount of time. _____ (Chapter 12)

    A. for two years

    B. for three months

    C. since childhood

13. Mr. Bumble became master of the workhouse and became sterner than ever. What does sterner mean? _____ (Chapter 13)

    A. strict and harsh

    B. kind and forgiving

    C. jovial and happy

14. Oliver's mother left a gold locket, but something was unusual about it. _____ (Chapter 14)

    A. It only had her first name, Agnes, with a blank space for the last name.

    B. It had Agnes as the first name, and that was not her name.

    C. It had Agnes on it, and they hoped it would say Marybeth.

15. Adjectives are words that describe nouns. What are some adjectives to describe Bill Sikes? _____ (Chapter 15)

    A. clean and neat

    B. dirty and bearded

    C. cheerful and humorous

16. What are some adjectives to describe Nancy? _____ (Chapter 15)

    A. sad and scared

    B. humorous and happy

    C. angry and mean

17. Why did Noah Claypole let his girlfriend Charlotte carry the heavy bag of money? _____ (Chapter 17)

    A. to strengthen her muscles

    B. to teach her a lesson

    C. to let her go to jail and not him in case they were caught

18. Fagin had a sly smile. What kind smile was a sly one? _____ (Chapter 18)

    A. sneaky

    B. very friendly

    C. forced

19. Why did Nancy really want to go out at 11:00 at night? _____ (Chapter 19)

    A. to get some fresh air

    B. to meet Rose Maylie as planned

    C. to go shopping

20. Who was listening when Nancy talked to Rose Maylie and Mr. Brownlow? _____ (Chapter 20)

    A. Fagin

    B. Monks

    C. Noah

21. Why was poor Nancy murdered? _____ (Chapter 21)

    A. Sikes found out about her midnight conversation.

    B. Sikes thought she was an intruder.

    C. Sikes' gun went off accidentally.

22. Mr. Brownlow called Monks this. _____ (Chapter 22)

    A. a foolish clown and a comedian

    B. an unworthy son, a coward, and a liar

    C. a lazy, good-for-nothing bum

23. A picture can tell a story. If your version of the book has a picture on page 214, what words describe the picture? (Look at the picture on page 214 to answer this question.) _____ (Chapter 23)

    A. an elegant, tidy home

    B. a country estate

    C. a broken-down filthy mess

24. Oliver Twist had a rough childhood, but now things would be different because of this. _____ (Chapter 25)

    A. He went to live with his real father.

    B. He inherited a lot of money, and Mr. Brownlow adopted him.

    C. He would live with Fagin and the gang.

25. Oliver's brother Monks had half of the money, and he did this. _____
(Chapter 25)

      A. He squandered his share and soon returned to a life of crime.

      B. He went to live with Oliver.

      C. He became a millionaire.

You can find the answers to these questions on page 99.

LITERATURE GUIDE THREE

The Lion, the Witch and the Wardrobe

by C. S. Lewis

Chapter Questions

Student Instructions: Read the book and answer the questions as you finish each chapter. If you need help, you may look in the book for help.

1. What surprise did Lucy find when she stepped into the wardrobe to feel the fur coats? _____ (Chapter 1)

    A. It led to a snow-covered land.

    B. It led to another bedroom.

    C. It led to a series of stairs.

2. What did the fawn, Mr. Tumnus, do to Lucy? _____ (Chapter 2)

    A. He took her to the White Witch.

    B. He led her safely back to the wardrobe.

    C. He took her to the lion.

3. What did Edmund discover about Lucy's imaginary country? _____ (Chapter 3)

    A. She was not imagining it at all.

    B. She was only dreaming.

    C. He was also dreaming.

4. What was so unusual about the Turkish Delight the White Witch gave Edmund? _____ (Chapter 4)

    A. It was really hot chocolate.

    B. Anyone who tasted it would never want any more.

    C. Anyone who tasted it would want more and more of it.

5. When Lucy and Edmund were both back in the house with Susan and Peter, what did Edmund do? _____ (Chapter 5)

    A. He said, "Lucy and I were only pretending."

    B. He said, "Lucy and I saw Mr. Tumnus."

    C. He said, "We should all go into the wardrobe."

6. Mr. Tumnus was arrested and charged with this. _____ (Chapter 6)

    A. high treason against the queen

    B. harboring spies

    C. both A and B

7. Why was the beaver afraid of speaking loudly around the trees? _____ (Chapter 7)

    A. The trees could amplify sounds.

    B. The trees could hear, and some of them would betray them.

    C. The trees were going to be cut down for firewood.

8. How did Mrs. Beaver know Edmund had been with the witch? _____ (Chapter 8)

    A. something about his eyes

    B. something about his smile

    C. something about his voice

9. When Edmund went to the White Witch's house, he noticed these. _____ (Chapter 9)

    A. several children making snowmen

    B. several dogs and puppies

    C. several white stone statues

10. Whom was Mr. Beaver so happy to see? _____ (Chapter10)

    A. Mr. Beaver's father

    B. Father Christmas

    C. Lucy's father

11. Something wonderful started happening. What was it? _____ (Chapter 11)

    A. Spring was coming and winter would be over.

    B. It started snowing more, and they would be able to go faster on the sledge.

    C. Edmund joined the squirrel and foxes at their party.

12. Peter had his first battle with what? _____ (Chapter 12)

    A. a bear

    B. a lion

    C. a wolf

13. Aslan agreed to meet with the Queen of Narnia on the condition she would leave this at the great oak. _____ (Chapter 13)

    A. her wolves

    B. her dwarfs

    C. her wand

14. What happened to Aslan? _____ (Chapter 14)

    A. He was shaved.

    B. He was killed.

    C. Both A and B

15. Why didn't the Witch realize Aslan could come back to life? _____ (Chapter 15)

    A. She knew the deep magic, but she did not know the "deeper" magic.

    B. She knew the deep magic but did not really kill him.

    C. She knew the deep magic but didn't want to kill him.

16. What happened to Peter, Susan, Edmund, and Lucy in this last chapter? _____ (Chapter 16)

    A. They became kings and queens.

    B. They went back into the wardrobe and returned to the professor's house.

    C. Both A and B

Student, when you've checked and corrected all your answers in this literature guide and you've read every page in the book, then take the End of the Book Test.

You can find the answers to these questions on page 100.

The Lion, the Witch and the Wardrobe

by C. S. Lewis

End of the Book Test

Student Instructions: Student, each question is worth 4 points. Let's see how well you've read this book. You may use this as an open book test and complete it within a 30-minute time limit. After you take the test, have your teacher/parent score the test for you. Then correct the wrong answers by reviewing the book for the correct answers.

1. Why were the four children sent away from London? _____ (Chapter 1)

   A. There were air raids in London.

   B. They were on vacation.

   C. Their parents were ill.

2. What did Lucy find strange about the lamp post? _____ (Chapter 1)

   A. Lamp posts are not usually in the woods.

   B. Lamp posts are usually red.

   C. Lamp posts are usually turned off.

3. Why was Mr. Tumnus crying? _____ (Chapter 2)

   A. He was very sorry for pretending to be Lucy's friend.

   B. He was sorry he had taken service under the White Witch.

   C. Both A and B

4. Why didn't Peter and the others miss Lucy when she was gone to Narnia? _____ (Chapter 3)

   A. They were too busy to miss her.

   B. They said she was only gone a moment.

   C. They were angry with her.

5. The Queen of Narnia, also called the White Witch, told Edmund he would become the King of Narnia. Why did she tell him that? _____ (Chapter 4)

   A. She was convinced he would be an excellent king because he was a Son of Adam.

   B. She was tricking him so he would be loyal to her and return to her with his brother and sisters.

   C. Neither A nor B

6. The Turkish Delight the Queen gave Edmund was this. _____ (Chapter 4)

   A. It was enchanted and delicious.

   B. It could cause a person to want to keep eating until they killed themselves.

   C. Both A and B

7. Why did all four children go into the wardrobe? _____ (Chapter 5)

    A. to hide from the professor because he was angry with them

    B. to hide from Mrs. Macready and a sightseeing gang

    C. to look for some fur coats

8. For which prophecy was the White Witch concerned? _____ (Chapter 8)

    A. Two sons of Adam and two daughters of Eve would sit on four thrones.

    B. Two sons of Adam and two daughters of Eve would not survive a trip to Narnia.

    C. Neither A nor B

9. Mr. Beaver said this about Aslan. _____ (Chapter 8)

    A. "He is very safe and very good."

    B. "He isn't safe, but he's good."

    C. "He isn't safe, and he isn't good."

10. Mrs. Beaver told the children the White Witch would use Edmund as a decoy. What does decoy mean in this sentence? _____ (Chapter 8)

    A. The White Witch would use Edmund to go hunting.

    B. The White Witch would use Edmund to trick the other children into going to her.

    C. The White Witch would be nice to Edmund and adopt him as her son some day.

11. Was the White Witch human? _____ (Chapter 8)

    A. The White Witch was human.

    B. The White Witch was not human.

    C. The White Witch was half human.

12. Hearing about Aslan gave Edmund a mysterious and horrible feeling but gave the other children a mysterious and lovely feeling. Why did Edmund feel differently about Aslan? _____ (Chapter 9)

    A. Edmund had eaten the White Witch's magic Turkish Delight.

    B. Edmund just didn't like lions and didn't want to see one.

    C. Neither A nor B

13. What did Edmund want to have happen to his brother and sisters? _____ (Chapter 9)

    A. He wanted the White Witch to turn them into stone.

    B. He didn't want the White Witch to turn them into stone.

    C. He wanted the White Witch to make them all beavers.

14. Why was everyone getting impatient with Mrs. Beaver when they were leaving their home to escape from the White Witch? _____ (Chapter 10)

    A. Mrs. Beaver wanted to pack food for them to take with them, and it was taking a long time.

    B. Mrs. Beaver wanted to take her sewing machine with them, and that would have taken too much time.

    C. Both A and B

15. Father Christmas gave the children presents, but he said they were not toys. He said they were _____. (Chapter 10)

    A. tools

    B. food

    C. clothes

16. The White Witch saw some animals sitting on stools and having a party. She was very angry and said, "What's the meaning of this?" Then she turned them into _____. (Chapter 11)

    A. squirrels

    B. stone figures

    C. wolves

17. Why was it winter for so long in Narnia? _____ (Chapter 12)

    A. The lion kept it that way.

    B. The witch put a spell on the land and kept it that way.

    C. A wicked meteorologist kept it that way.

18. How did Peter feel when he first battled with the wolf? _____ (Chapter 12)

    A. Peter did not feel brave.

    B. Peter felt like he was going to be sick.

    C. Both A and B

19. The White Witch said this about Edmund. _____ (Chapter 13)

    A. He was a traitor, and all traitors belonged to her.

    B. He was a nice boy, and she wanted him to live in her castle.

    C. He was free to do whatever he wanted.

20. Why did Aslan allow himself to be killed? _____ (Chapter 14)

    A. to sacrifice himself for the others

    B. to put an end to the White Witch's spell

    C. both A and B

21. The girls were crying when they saw Aslan dead and tied up. They tried to untie the cords, but they couldn't. How did the cords get off Aslan? _____ (Chapter 15)

    A. Hundreds of little field mice gnawed the ropes.

    B. Peter helped them untie them.

    C. They used a sharp knife to cut them.

22. With the rising of the sun, the girls saw that the Stone Tablet was broken in two pieces, and Aslan was gone. Where was Aslan? _____ (Chapter 15)

    A. Aslan's body was taken away by the White Witch.

    B. Aslan came back to life.

    C. Aslan was buried.

23. How did the statues come back to life? _____ (Chapter 16)

    A. Aslan breathed on them.

    B. Aslan waved a magic wand.

    C. Aslan sprayed water on them.

24. Who finally killed the witch? _____ (Chapter 16)

    A. Aslan

    B. Peter

    C. Edmund

25. What helped Edmund and others who were wounded in the final battle? _____ (Chapter 17)

    A. Lucy's cordial

    B. Lucy's tea

    C. Lucy's handkerchief

You can find the answers to these questions on page 101.

LITERATURE GUIDE FOUR

A Christmas Carol
by Charles Dickens

Chapter Questions

Student Instructions: Read the book and answer the questions as you finish each chapter. If you need help, you may look in the book for help.

1. No one ever stopped to talk to Ebenezer Scrooge. Everyone stayed away from him. How did he feel about this? _____ (Chapter 1)

    A. He wished they would be friendlier to him.

    B. He actually liked this.

    C. He tried to make friends.

2. Scrooge's nephew, Fred, came to wish Scrooge a Merry Christmas. How did Scrooge react? _____ (Chapter 2)

    A. He wished Fred a Merry Christmas.

    B. He gave Fred a present.

    C. He said he wouldn't care if Christmas never came again.

3. When two men came to Scrooge to ask for money for poor people, what did Scrooge say about poor people? _____ (Chapter 2)

    A. Let them die.

    B. Let them live.

    C. Let them get gifts.

4. Scrooge ate at his usual tavern and had his usual, melancholy dinner. What does melancholy mean? _____ (Chapter 3)

    A. joyful

    B. meaningful

    C. sad

5. The ghost of Marley was dragging some chains. What did those chains represent? _____ (Chapter 3)

    A. his selfishness and lack of generosity

    B. his desire to make noise

    C. his kindness to the poor

6. What happened to Scrooge as a child that made him dislike Christmas? _____ (Chapter 4)

   A. He was left at school and neglected by his family.

   B. He was spoiled by getting too many gifts.

   C. He was very sick on Christmas.

7. Scrooge's girlfriend broke off their engagement because she said Scrooge loved this more than her. _____ (Chapter 4)

   A. another girl

   B. traveling to foreign countries

   C. gold

8. Scrooge saw an attractive young girl who looked like his old girlfriend, Bell. Who was she? _____ (Chapter 4)

   A. Bell's daughter

   B. his sister, all grown up

   C. a stranger

9. How did the eyes of the Ghost of Christmas Present look? _____ (Chapter 5)

   A. mean and scary

   B. friendly and kind

   C. dull and sad

10. Had Scrooge learned a valuable lesson from being with the Ghost of Christmas Past? _____ (Chapter 5)

    A. yes

    B. no

11. Although the Ghost of Christmas Present was invisible to others in the story, he helped people with this. _____ (Chapter 5)

    A. his hat

    B. his sword

    C. his torch

12. Scrooge met Tiny Tim and found out this about him. _____ (Chapter 5)

    A. Tiny Tim might run away.

    B. Tiny Tim might die.

    C. Tiny Tim might get better.

13. The Ghost of Christmas Present reminded Scrooge he used to say this about poor unfortunate creatures. _____ (Chapter 5)

    A. It would be better if they died.

    B. It would be better if they were rich.

    C. It would be better if they helped each other.

14. Scrooge went to Fred's house and noticed this about his nephew and his family. _____ (Chapter 5)

    A. They were so happy.

    B. They were so mean.

    C. They were so lonely.

15. How did the Ghost of Christmas Yet to Come look? _____ (Chapter 6)

    A. He looked dark and scary.

    B. He looked light and friendly.

    C. He looked cute and cuddly.

16. Scrooge said he hoped to do this. _____ (Chapter 6)

    A. Scrooge hoped to be a better man than he was in the past.

    B. Scrooge hoped to be as mean and stingy as ever.

    C. Scrooge hoped to be a Christmas ghost.

17. The Ghost of Christmas Yet to Come showed Scrooge this would happen to little Tiny Tim in the future. _____ (Chapter 6)

    A. Tiny Tim would run away.

    B. Tiny Tim would die.

    C. Tiny Tim would laugh.

18. The Ghost of Christmas Yet to Come showed Ebenezer Scrooge someone's grave at the cemetery. Whose grave was it? _____ (Chapter 6)

    A. Marley's grave

    B. Fred's grave

    C. his own grave, Ebenezer Scrooge

19. Ebenezer Scrooge woke up on Christmas Day and realized he was back home. He also realized he was given a second chance, so he was _____ (Chapter 7)

    A. happy

    B. sad

    C. angry

20. At the end of this story, how did Ebenezer Scrooge act? _____ (Chapters 8, 9)

    A. He was still mean and not generous.

    B. He liked Christmas and was kind to everyone.

    C. He just wanted to stay home alone.

Student, when you've checked and corrected all your answers in this literature guide and you've read every page in the book, then take the End of the Book Test.

You can find the answers to these questions on page 102.

A Christmas Carol

by Charles Dickens

End of the Book Test

Student Instructions: Student, each question is worth 4 points. Let's see how well you've read this book. You may use this as an open book test and complete it within a 30-minute time limit. After you take the test, have your teacher/parent score the test for you. Then correct the wrong answers by reviewing the book for the correct answers.

1. Ebenezer Scrooge was Marley's only mourner. What does mourner mean? _____ (Chapter 1)

    A. someone who gets up early in the morning

    B. someone who is sad when someone dies

    C. someone who doesn't like mornings

2. Two gentlemen wanted Ebenezer Scrooge to donate money for poor people. They asked if Scrooge wanted to give but remain anonymous. What does anonymous mean? _____ (Chapter 2)

    A. rewarded

    B. generous

    C. not giving your name

3. Why was Ebenezer Scrooge's dinner described as being melancholy? _____ (Chapter 3)

    A. He was always eating alone.

    B. He was eating an expensive meal.

    C. He was eating a cheap meal.

4. Marley's ghost was transparent. What does transparent mean? _____ (Chapter 3)

    A. see-through

    B. thick

    C. in constant motion

5. How did Ebenezer Scrooge react when he saw the countryside where he was born? _____ (Chapter 4)

    A. He thought it was foolish to be there.

    B. His lips trembled, and a tear was on his cheek.

    C. He felt angry and bitter.

6. Who were Ebenezer Scrooge's friends when his family and friends deserted him? _____ (Chapter 4)

   A. Facebook friends

   B. his childhood book friends

   C. the chickens and squirrels

7. What happened to Ebenezer Scrooge's sister? _____ (Chapter 4)

   A. She grew to be an old lady.

   B. She stayed single all her life.

   C. She got married, had one son named Fred, and then died.

8. Whose Christmas party did Ebenezer Scrooge go to when he was a young man? _____ (Chapter 4)

   A. his boss, Mr. Fezziwig

   B. his boss, Mr. Wilkins

   C. his boss, Mr. Dickens

9. Who was the attractive matron sitting opposite her daughter? _____ (Chapter 4)

   A. Ebenezer's sister

   B. Ebenezer's old girlfriend

   C. Ebenezer's niece

10. What did Ebenezer Scrooge say when the Ghost of Christmas Past showed him more of his past? _____ (Chapter 4)

    A. Ebenezer said, "I cannot bear it."

    B. Ebenezer said, "Thanks, Buddy."

    C. Ebenezer said, "Can I go back there again?"

11. How had Ebenezer Scrooge's sitting room changed when the Ghost of Christmas Present was there? _____ (Chapter 5)

    A. It became dark and gloomy.

    B. It had Christmas decorations and food.

    C. It was filled with many people.

12. How was Tiny Tim's hand described? _____ (Chapter 5)

    A. withered and little

    B. chubby and firm

    C. large and strong

13. How did Mrs. Cratchit describe Ebenezer Scrooge? _____ (Chapter 5)

    A. old, thin, tall, and funny

    B. strong, tall, thin, and professional

    C. stingy, hard, hateful, and unfeeling

14. Ebenezer Scrooge's nephew, Fred, said this about Scrooge. _____ (Chapter 5)

    A. I'm angry with him.

    B. I don't feel sorry for him.

    C. I feel sorry for him.

15. The Ghost of Christmas Present warned Scrooge to beware of these. _____ (Chapter 5)

    A. greed and pride

    B. pride and ignorance

    C. ignorance and greed

16. This is another name for the spirit or ghost. _____ (Chapter 6)

    A. grave

    B. phantom

    C. robe

17. How was the Ghost of Christmas Yet to Come different from the other ghosts? _____ (Chapter 6)

    A. He was friendlier.

    B. He was a child.

    C. He did not speak.

18. Whose funeral was going to take place on Sunday? _____ (Chapter 6)

    A. Tiny Tim's funeral

    B. Ebenezer's funeral

    C. Mrs. Cratchit's funeral

19. The memory of Tiny Tim influenced others in this way. We should stop and think twice before we do this _____ (Chapter 6)

    A. quarrel

    B. eat

    C. sing

20. If the Ghost of Christmas Yet to Come did not talk, how did he let Ebenezer Scrooge know where to go? _____ (Chapter 6)

    A. by writing on a tablet

    B. by looking in the direction

    C. by pointing with his finger

21. A desperate Ebenezer Scrooge asked the Ghost of Christmas Yet to Come this question. _____ (Chapter 6)

    A. Am I past all hope?

    B. Am I past all joy?

    C. Am I past all trouble?

22. Ebenezer Scrooge had changed, and he promised this. _____ (Chapter 6)

    A. I will honor Christmas in my heart.

    B. I will never see a ghost again.

    C. I will never come to this cemetery again.

23. Why did Scrooge get down on his knees? _____ (Chapter 7)

    A. to feel the bedpost

    B. to show he was grateful for a second chance

    C. to see if Jacob Marley's ghost was still there

24. What are some things Scrooge did when he realized he was given a second chance? _____ (Chapter 7)

   A. He bought a turkey for the Cratchit family.

   B. He went to church.

   C. Both A and B

25. The new Ebenezer Scrooge was this. _____ (Chapter 9)

   A. like a second father to Tiny Tim

   B. a good citizen, a good friend, and a good boss

   C. both A and B.

You can find the answers to these questions on page 103.

LITERATURE GUIDE FIVE

20,000 Leagues Under the Sea

by Jules Verne

Chapter Questions

Student Instructions: Read the book and answer the questions as you finish each chapter. If you need help, you may look in the book for help.

1. This book is written in what point of view? _____ (Chapter 1)

    A. first person – I, my, me

    B. second person – you, your

    C. third person – he/she, him/her

2. Monsieur Professor Pierre Aronnax told this story. He was an author and an expert on undersea life. He was on the ship to find the monster, and with him was Ned Land. Who was Ned? _____ (Chapter 2)

    A. an expert swimmer

    B. an expert harpooner

    C. an expert seafood cook

3. When Professor Aronnax, Conseil, and Ned were thrown into the water, they landed on a "floating island." What was this floating island? _____ (Chapter 3)

    A. an underwater boat bolted together with steel plates

    B. a small island with coconut trees

    C. an inflatable row boat with oars

4. Captain Nemo could speak English. Why didn't he speak to them before? _____ (Chapter 4)

    A. Captain Nemo said their cannons shot at them, so he couldn't trust them.

    B. Captain Nemo wasn't very good at languages and didn't understand them.

    C. Captain Nemo was busy hunting whales and decided not to talk to them.

5. The name of chapter five is the Remarkable Nautilus. What was so remarkable about it? _____ (Chapter 5)

    A. It could float and also fly in the sky.

    B. It was like a museum and a great library.

    C. It was well-known to scientists around the world.

6. How were they able to leave the underwater ship and breathe in the ocean? _____ (Chapter 6)

    A. They wore special suits and strapped air tanks on their backs.

    B. They kept swimming to the surface to get air.

    C. They only went under water for a few seconds.

7. Why wasn't Captain Nemo worried when the savages tried to get into the Nautilus? _____ (Chapter 7)

    A. He had electrically-charged ladders that shocked the savages.

    B. He knew sharks would get the savages first.

    C. He planned to get the Nautilus away before the savages could reach the ladders.

8. What did Aronnax find unusual about their next underwater excursion? _____ (Chapter 8)

    A. They were surrounded by whales.

    B. They found another submarine.

    C. They went to an underwater cemetery.

9. A shark opened its jaws and was ready to cut Captain Nemo in two, but then this happened. _____ (Chapter 9)

    A. Another shark came and fought with the shark.

    B. Ned Land harpooned the shark and struck its heart.

    C. Aronnax grabbed Captain Nemo and pulled him up safely to the dinghy.

10. Why was Ned concerned that they were heading into the Red Sea? _____ (Chapter 10)

    A. He didn't like the color red.

    B. He thought the water was too shallow.

    C. He knew the Suez Canal was not yet finished.

11. What was Ned's main goal? _____ (Chapter 11)

    A. to escape and have freedom

    B. to learn more about ocean life

    C. to steal some of Captain Nemo's gold

12. What did members of the Nautilus crew find on the ocean floor? _____ (Chapter 12)

      A. dead shark and whale bones

      B. coins, jewels, gold, and silver from Spanish ships

      C. Ned, Conseil, and Professor Aronnax

13. What was glowing red under the water? _____ (Chapter 13)

      A. red lava from an underwater volcano

      B. red blood from whales

      C. red seaweed

14. How did the Nautilus get to the South Pole when there were so many icebergs in the way? _____ (Chapter 14)

      A. They flew over the icebergs.

      B. They melted the icebergs with hot air guns.

      C. They went down below the icebergs.

15. They were in danger of running out of this. _____ (Chapter 15)

      A. water

      B. food

      C. air

16. Why did Captain Nemo cry? _____ (Chapter 16)

      A. One of his men was killed by a giant squid.

      B. Many giant squid died.

      C. He missed a chance to take a photograph of the squid.

17. What would Captain Nemo reveal in the book he was writing? _____ (Chapter 17)

      A. his plans to be happier living on land again

      B. his real name and the story of his life

      C. his plans to develop a submarine that could also fly

18. The Nautilus got caught in a maelstrom. What is a maelstrom? _____
    (Chapter 18)

       A. a violent wind

       B. a violent sailor

       C. a violent whirlpool

Student, when you've checked and corrected all your answers in this literature guide and you've read every page in the book, then take the End of the Book Test.

You can find the answers to these questions on page 104.

20,000 Leagues Under the Sea

by Jules Verne

End of the Book Test

Student Instructions: Student, each question is worth 4 points. Let's see how well you've read this book. You may use this as an open book test and complete it within a 30-minute time limit. After you take the test, have your teacher/parent score the test for you. Then correct the wrong answers by reviewing the book for the correct answers.

1. In chapter one, we learn that there had been many sightings of a mysterious monster in the oceans of the world. Monsieur Pierre Aronnax thought he solved the mystery of the sea monster when he believed it was a giant narwhal. What is a narwhal? _____ (Chapter 1)

    A. a kind of long whale with a hard tusk

    B. a kind of shark with spikes

    C. a creature from another planet

2. Why didn't Ned believe the sea monster was a narwhal? _____ (Chapter 2)

    A. Ned knew a narwhal's tusk was not strong enough to crack open a steel hull of a ship.

    B. Ned knew all about submarines and thought the sea monster was a submarine.

    C. Ned thought narwhals were only in fairy tales.

3. Why was everyone surprised the monster they were searching for was actually an underwater submarine vessel? _____ (Chapter 3)

    A. There were hundreds of submarines throughout all the oceans of the world at that time.

    B. Submarines had not yet been developed.

    C. Submarines were always painted yellow.

4. At first, Professor Aronnax thought Captain Nemo could not understand English because he would not respond to them. Why didn't Captain Nemo talk to them when they first met him? _____ (Chapter 4)

    A. Captain Nemo didn't trust them because they shot and harpooned the Nautilus.

    B. Captain Nemo liked playing guessing games.

    C. Captain Nemo was too busy hunting whales.

5. What was so remarkable about the Nautilus? _____ (Chapter 5)

    A. It was like a museum and great library.

    B. It was filled with many children and women.

    C. It was well-known to scientists around the world.

6. How were they able to leave the underwater ship and breathe in the ocean? _____ (Chapter 6)

    A. They had a mini-sub to ride in.

    B. They wore special suits and strapped air tanks on their backs.

    C. They kept swimming to the surface to get air.

7. Why were they so anxious to go on land? _____ (Chapter 6)

    A. They wanted to eat meat for a change.

    B. They wanted to eat fish for a change.

    C. They wanted to drive a car for a change.

8. Why wasn't Captain Nemo worried when savages tried to get into the Nautilus? _____ (Chapter 7)

    A. Captain Nemo had electrically-charged ladders that gave shocks.

    B. Captain Nemo thought the savages would be friendly and share their island.

    C. Captain Nemo knew sharks and squids would attack the savages first.

9. They went on another underwater expedition in their special outfits and air tanks. Why did they leave the ship this time? _____ (Chapter 8)

    A. They were hunting for whales.

    B. They wanted to find another submarine.

    C. They went to an underwater cemetery.

10. Who were they burying in the cemetery? _____ (Chapter 8)

    A. Captain Nemo

    B. Ned Land

    C. A crewman

11. A shark's jaws opened, ready to cut Captain Nemo in two, but then this happened. _____ (Chapter 9)

    A. Another shark came and fought with the shark.

    B. Ned Land harpooned the shark and struck its heart.

    C. Aronnax grabbed Captain Nemo and pulled him up safely to the dinghy.

12. Why was Ned concerned that they were heading into the Red Sea? _____ (Chapter 10)

    A. The Suez Canal was not yet finished, and there was no opening to go through.

    B. The Red Sea was a dangerous place with frequent storms.

    C. The Red Sea was too shallow.

13. What was Ned's main goal? _____ (Chapter 11)

    A. to escape and have freedom

    B. to learn more about ocean life

    C. to steal some of Captain Nemo's gold

14. Treasures of coins, gold, silver, and jewels were on the bottom of the sea. What kind of ships did they come from? _____ (Chapter 12)

    A. Spanish ships that lost a battle with the English

    B. English ships that lost a battle with the Spanish

    C. Italian ships that lost a battle with the Chinese

15. What was glowing red under the water? _____ (Chapter 13)

    A. red lava from an underwater volcano

    B. red blood from whales

    C. red seaweed

16. They found the sunken ruins of what continent? _____ (Chapter 13)

    A. Atlantis

    B. Avatar

    C. Australia

17. Why did Captain Nemo want to go to the South Pole? _____ (Chapter 14)

    A. to succeed at reaching it when others had failed

    B. to hunt playful black whales

    C. to find another lost continent

18. When they were trapped under the ice, they were in danger of running out of this. _____ (Chapter 15)

    A. water

    B. food

    C. air

19. What came out of the giant squid? _____ (Chapter 16)

    A. black ink

    B. white foam

    C. purple jell-like substance

20. Where did Captain Nemo plan to put his book? _____ (Chapter 17)

    A. in the underwater cemetery

    B. in a small unsinkable box

    C. in the belly of a giant fish

21. The Nautilus got caught in a maelstrom. What is a maelstrom? _____ (Chapter 18)

    A. a violent wind

    B. a violent sailor

    C. a violent whirlpool

22. Why did Ned and the others want to leave the Nautilus if it was so remarkable? _____ (Chapter 18)

  A. Captain Nemo said no one would ever leave, and they wanted their freedom.

  B. They wanted to finally get back to land after being at sea for so long.

  C. Both A and B

23. The distance of 20,000 leagues is equal to how many miles? _____ (Chapter 18)

  A. 600 miles

  B. 6,000 miles

  C. 60,000 miles

24. Was Captain Nemo still alive at the end of the story? _____ (Chapter 18)

  A. Yes, he was alive.

  B. No, he had died.

  C. We don't know if he was alive or dead.

25. The author, Jules Verne, wrote about submarines in this fictional book. What was so remarkable about this? _____ (From "About the Author" pages)

  A. Verne wrote about this thirty years before an actual ocean-going submarine was developed.

  B. Verne's fictional inventions were believable because he explained them with accurate scientific details.

  C. Both A and B

You can find the answers to these questions on page 105.

LITERATURE GUIDE SIX

Dark Enough to See the Stars

By Cindy Noonan

Chapter Questions

Student Instructions: Read the book and answer the questions as you finish each chapter. If you need help, you may look in the book for help.

1. The main character in this story was named Moses, or Mose, for short. How was he like Moses in the Bible? _____ (Chapter 1)

    A. Their mothers didn't want them to be slaves.

    B. They were both Egyptian slaves.

    C. They both floated in baskets as babies.

2. Why were Mose and his mother so sad at the beginning of this story? _____ (Chapter 1)

    A. They were both going on a long train ride.

    B. They were being separated.

    C. They had to both run in the woods to escape.

3. Mose's mother told him to follow the Drinkin' Gourd when it was dark. What did she mean? _____ (Chapter 1)

    A. Follow the Drinkin' Gourd to have plenty of water to drink.

    B. Follow the stars in a southern direction.

    C. Follow the North Star, which would lead him to freedom.

4. Mama told Moses about the Underground Railroad. What was the Underground Railroad? _____ (Chapter 3)

    A. A railroad which ran in an underground tunnel.

    B. A system of leading runaway slaves to safe locations.

    C. A railroad meant for carrying people and products across the country.

5. Why did Moses need to get north of the Mason-Dixon Line into Pennsylvania? _____ (Chapter 5)

    A. Pennsylvania was part of Canada.

    B. Pennsylvania was the location of Moses' mother.

    C. Pennsylvania was a free state.

6. Joel taught Moses to spell his name. What was so unusual about this? _____ (Chapter 6)

    A. Moses was a slave, and slaves were not allowed to read, write, or spell.

    B. Moses already knew how to spell his name.

    C. Moses had no interest in learning how to spell or write.

7. Moses had to ride in a "hidey-hole" in Miller Johnson's wagon. Why was it necessary for Moses to hide? _____ (Chapter 9)

    A. Slave catchers might see him and send him back to his owner.

    B. Moses wanted to be comfortable, so he chose to lie down rather than sit.

    C. Miller Johnson didn't like Moses and didn't want him sitting beside him.

8. Who wrote a free paper for Mose? _____ (Chapter 12)

    A. Mr. Stevens

    B. Mr. Dobbins

    C. Miller Johnson

9. Miz Palmer was so happy to be able to teach Moses along with Tillie. Where was their hidden "schoolhouse?" _____ (Chapter 15)

    A. in an attic

    B. in a cellar

    C. in a cave

10. The Fugitive Slave Act required everyone to assist slave catchers. If anyone fed or housed an escaped slave, they would have to do this. _____ (Chapter 16)

    A. Pay a thousand-dollar fine.

    B. Spend six months in prison.

    C. Both A and B

11. Who tried to attack Tillie when she was in the boat? _____ (Chapter 21)

    A. Robert

    B. Jeb

    C. Daniel

12. What signal did Katie Jane use to show escaped slaves it was safe to cross Lycoming Creek? _____ (Chapter 23)

    A. one lantern

    B. two lanterns

    C. no lantern

13. Moses and Tillie had to ride in Dr. Smith's carriage under a canvas along with bags of flour and corn. Why did they still have to hide? _____ (Chapter 26)

    A. The sheriff or a bounty hunter might see them.

    B. That "horrible law," the Fugitive Slave Act

    C. Both A and B

14. What did Mose find unusual about being in a church with smooth, dark wood benches or "pews?" _____ (Chapter 27)

    A. Moses had only been to outdoor camp meetings and had never been in a church.

    B. Moses was used to fancier, more elaborate churches in the South.

15. Why was Moses fearful of meeting a pastor named Reverend White? _____ (Chapter 27)

    A. He thought Reverend White would be white, not black.

    B. The white pastors Moses met told slaves to obey their masters.

    C. Both A and B

16. Why were Moses and Tillie given clean, nice clothes to wear? _____ (Chapter 29)

    A. People would believe they were the mayor's servants.

    B. No one would suspect they were runaways.

    C. Both A and B

17. Moses and Tillie hid in a hole with bags and boxes under the boiler in the ship. Who was trying to find them? _____ (Chapter 30)

    A. Frank

    B. Jeb

    C. Sam

18. Moses and Tillie narrowly escaped in a horse and buggy and finally made it to Lockport, New York. From there, how did they travel to the border of Canada? _____ (Chapter 36)

    A. on a train filled with mailbags

    B. on a ship filled with mailbags

    C. on a stagecoach filled with mailbags

19. What happened to Tillie? _____ (Chapter 37)

    A. Jeb and Tillie went back south.

    B. Jeb and Tillie fell off the bridge.

    C. Jeb and Tillie were shot.

20. In the final chapter of this book, the setting is three months later. Now Moses is doing this. _____ (Chapter 38)

    A. Moses is going to school and doing chores for the Bibbs.

    B. Moses plans to write about slavery and be an abolitionist.

    C. Both A and B

Student, when you've checked and corrected all your answers in this literature guide and you've read every page in the book, then take the End of the Book Test.

You can find the answers to these questions on page 106.

Dark Enough to See the Stars

By Cindy Noonan

End of the Book Test

<u>Student Instructions</u>: Student, each question is worth 4 points. Let's see how well you've read this book. You may use this as an open book test and complete it within a 30-minute time limit. After you take the test, have your teacher/parent score the test for you. Then correct the wrong answers by reviewing the book for the correct answers.

1. The main character in this story was named Moses, or Mose, for short. How was he like Moses in the Bible? _____ (Chapter 1)

   A. Their mothers didn't want them to be slaves.

   B. They were both Egyptian slaves.

   C. They both floated in baskets as babies.

2. Moses and his mother were slaves, and their master was Masta Bill. Masta Bill was selling Mama but keeping Moses. Why was he keeping Moses? _____ (Chapter 1)

   A. Masta Bill said Moses could chop wood faster than any darkie on the plantation.

   B. Masta Bill said Moses was as strong as his best mule.

   C. Both A and B

3. Moses' mother told him to follow the Drinkin'Gourd when it was dark. What did she mean? _____ (Chapter 1)

   A. Follow the Drinkin' Gourd to have plenty of water to drink.

   B. Follow the stars in a southern direction.

   C. Follow the North Star which would lead him to freedom.

4. Mama told Moses about the Underground Railroad. What was the Underground Railroad? _____ (Chapter 3)

   A. A railroad which ran in an underground tunnel.

   B. A system of leading runaway slaves to safe locations.

   C. A railroad meant for carrying people and products across the country.

5. Moses was chased by dogs, but what happened to make them lose his trail? _____ (Chapter 3)

   A. The dogs smelled a skunk.

   B. The dogs chased a cat instead.

   C. The dogs fell in a pond.

6. Why did Mose need to get north of the Mason-Dixon Line into Pennsylvania? _____ (Chapter 5)

    A. Pennsylvania was part of Canada.

    B. Pennsylvania was the location of Moses' mother.

    C. Pennsylvania was a free state.

7. Joel taught Mose to spell his name. What was so unusual about this? _____ (Chapter 6)

    A. Moses was a slave, and slaves were not allowed to read, write, or spell.

    B. Moses already knew how to spell his name.

    C. Moses had no interest in learning how to spell or write.

8. Moses had to ride in a "hidey-hole" in Miller Johnson's wagon. Why was it necessary for Moses to hide? _____ (Chapter 9)

    A. Slave catchers might see him and send him back to his owner.

    B. Moses wanted to be comfortable, so he chose to lie down rather than sit.

    C. Miller Johnson didn't like Moses and didn't want him sitting beside him.

9. Who wrote a free paper for Mose? _____ (Chapter 12)

    A. Mr. Stevens

    B. Mr. Dobbins

    C. Miller Johnson

10. What happened to Moses' free paper? _____ (Chapter 13)

    A. It burned, and the words were unreadable.

    B. It got wet from rain, and the words were smeared.

    C. It was torn and unreadable.

11. Miz Palmer was so happy to be able to teach Moses along with Tillie. Where was their hidden "schoolhouse?" _____ (Chapter 15)

   A. in an attic

   B. in a cellar

   C. in a cave

12. The Fugitive Slave Act required everyone to assist slave catchers. If anyone fed or housed an escaped slave, they would have to do this? _____ (Chapter 16)

   A. Pay a thousand-dollar fine.

   B. Spend six months in prison.

   C. Both A and B

13. How is Daniel Hughes described? _____ (Chapter 18)

   A. tall, half black, and half Indian who helped fugitives

   B. short with red hair and a red beard, who helped slave catchers

   C. neither A nor B

14. Moses and Tillie had an encounter with wolves. How did they defend themselves? _____ (Chapter 19)

   A. They hid in a "hidey-hole" in an old log.

   B. They yelled and used stick and rocks to hit the wolves.

   C. They climbed a tree.

15. Who tried to attack Tillie when she was in the boat? _____ (Chapter 21)

   A. Robert

   B. Jeb

   C. Daniel

16. What signal did Katie Jane use to show escaped slaves it was safe to cross Lycoming Creek? _____ (Chapter 23)

   A. one lantern

   B. two lanterns

   C. no lantern

17. Moses and Tillie had to ride in Dr. Smith's carriage under a canvas along with bags of flour and corn. Why did they still have to hide? _____ (Chapter 26)

    A. The sheriff or a bounty hunter might see them.

    B. That "horrible law," the Fugitive Slave Act

    C. Both A and B

18. What was unusual about being in a church with smooth, dark wood benches or "pews?" _____ (Chapter 27)

    A. Moses had only been to outdoor camp meetings and had never been in a church.

    B. Moses was used to fancier, more elaborate churches in the South.

19. Why was Moses fearful of meeting a pastor named Reverend White? _____ (Chapter 27)

    A. He thought Reverend White would be white, not black.

    B. White pastors he met told slaves to obey their masters.

    C. Both A and B

20. Why were Moses and Tillie given clean, nice clothes to wear? _____ (Chapter 29)

    A. People would believe they were the mayor's servants.

    B. No one would suspect they were runaways.

    C. Both A and B

21. Moses and Tillie hid in a hole with bags and boxes under the boiler in the ship. Who was trying to find them? _____ (Chapter 30)

    A. Frank

    B. Jeb

    C. Sam

22. After their train ride, Moses and Tillie went to the print shop of Frederick Douglas who encouraged Moses. He said one day Moses may do this. _____ (Chapter 32)

    A. Moses could be a captain on a ship.

    B. Moses could be a conductor on a train.

    C. Moses could write articles for the newspaper.

23. Moses and Tillie narrowly escaped in a horse and buggy, but they finally made it to Lockport, New York. From there, they traveled to the border of Canada in a _____ (Chapter 36)

    A. train filled with mailbags

    B. ship filled with mailbags

    C. stagecoach filled with mailbags

24. What happened to Tillie? _____ (Chapter 37)

    A. Jeb and Tillie went back south.

    B. Jeb and Tillie fell off the bridge.

    C. Jeb and Tillie were shot.

25. In the final chapter of this book, the setting is three months later. Now Moses is doing this. _____ (Chapter 38)

    A. Moses is going to school and doing chores for the Bibbs.

    B. Moses plans to write about slavery and be an abolitionist.

    C. Both A and

You can find the answers to these questions on page 107.

Student, this now completes your six-book set. Congratulations!

Look for more exciting adventures with literature guides

From Carolyn Oravitz.

Answer Sheets

ROBINSON CRUSOE

BY DANIEL DEFOE

Chapter Questions

1.	A	14.	C
2.	B	15.	A
3.	A	16.	B
4.	B	17.	A
5.	A	18.	C
6.	A	19.	B
7.	C	20.	A
8.	B	21.	A
9.	A	22.	A
10.	A	23.	B
11.	C	24.	A
12.	B	25.	C
13.	B		

ROBINSON CRUSOE
BY DANIEL DEFOE

END OF THE BOOK TEST

1. A
2. C
3. B
4. A
5. A
6. C
7. A
8. A
9. B
10. C
11. B
12. A
13. C

14. A
15. A
16. A
17. C
18. B
19. A
20. A
21. C
22. C
23. C
24. A
25. B

OLIVER TWIST
BY CHARLES DICKENS

CHAPTER QUESTIONS

1. A
2. B
3. A
4. B
5. C
6. A
7. C
8. A
9. B
10. C
11. A
12. A
13. C

14. B
15. C
16. A
17. A
18. C
19. B
20. C
21. C
22. A
23. B
24. C
25. A

OLIVER TWIST
BY CHARLES DICKENS

END OF THE BOOK TEST

1. A
2. B
3. A
4. C
5. B
6. B
7. A
8. B
9. A
10. C
11. B
12. C
13. A

14. A
15. B
16. A
17. C
18. A
19. B
20. C
21. A
22. B
23. C
24. B
25. A

THE LION, THE WITCH AND THE WARDROBE
BY C. S. LEWIS

CHAPTER QUESTIONS

1. A
2. B
3. A
4. C
5. A
6. C
7. B
8. A

9. C
10. B
11. A
12. C
13. C
14. C
15. A
16. C

THE LION, THE WITCH AND THE WARDROBE

BY C. S. LEWIS

END OF THE BOOK TEST

1. A		14.	C
2. A		15.	A
3. C		16.	B
4. B		17.	B
5. B		18.	C
6. C		19.	A
7. B		20.	C
8. A		21.	A
9. B		22.	B
10. B		23.	A
11. C		24.	A
12. A		25.	A
13. B			

A CHRISTMAS CAROL
BY CHARLES DICKENS

CHAPTER QUESTIONS

1. B
2. C
3. A
4. C
5. A
6. A
7. C
8. A
9. B
10. A

11. C
12. B
13. A
14. A
15. A
16. A
17. B
18. C
19. A
20. B

A CHRISTMAS CAROL
BY CHARLES DICKENS

END OF THE BOOK TEST

1. B
2. C
3. A
4. A
5. B
6. B
7. C
8. A
9. B
10. A
11. B
12. A
13. C

14. C
15. A
16. B
17. C
18. A
19. A
20. C
21. A
22. A
23. B
24. C
25. C

20,000 LEAGUES
UNDER THE SEA
BY JULES VERNE

CHAPTER QUESTIONS

1. A
2. B
3. A
4. A
5. B
6. A
7. A
8. C
9. B

10. C
11. A
12. B
13. A
14. C
15. C
16. A
17. B
18. C

20,000 LEAGUES UNDER THE SEA
BY JULES VERNE

END OF THE BOOK TEST

1. A
2. A
3. B
4. A
5. A
6. B
7. A
8. A
9. C
10. C
11. B
12. A
13. A

14. A
15. A
16. A
17. A
18. C
19. A
20. B
21. C
22. C
23. C
24. C
25. C

DARK ENOUGH TO SEE THE STARS

BY CINDY NOONAN

CHAPTER QUESTIONS

1.	A		11.	B
2.	B		12.	B
3.	C		13.	C
4.	B		14.	A
5.	C		15.	C
6.	A		16.	C
7.	A		17.	B
8.	A		18.	C
9.	B		19.	B
10.	C		20.	C

DARK ENOUGH TO SEE THE STARS
BY CINDY NOONAN

END OF THE BOOK TEST

1. A
2. C
3. C
4. B
5. A
6. C
7. A
8. A
9. A
10. B
11. B
12. C
13. A

14. B
15. B
16. B
17. C
18. A
19. C
20. C
21. B
22. C
23. C
24. B
25. C

Student, this now completes your six-book set. Congratulations!

Look for more exciting adventures with literature guides from Carolyn Oravitz.

ABOUT THE AUTHOR

Author Carolyn Oravitz - With 30 years of teaching experience and certificates in both elementary education and high school English, author Carolyn Oravitz brings a wealth of experience in teaching reading. Her literature guides are designed to motivate children to develop a love for reading while developing the necessary reading comprehension and vocabulary skills to succeed.